TOO BUSY TO LIVE YOUR LIFE?

Take another look and walk with joy

28 days

to see Nature in a completely different light

Joy Davies

Walk with Joy

How often do you think 'I really wish I had more time to…'?

Are you always thinking about the next task rather than enjoying the one you are doing? Do you ever stop to breathe? Do you think it's all going to get better after Christmas or when you've been on holiday, when you get a new job or when the children leave home? Do you ever think what's this (Life) all about, where am I going, and will I ever get there — wherever 'there' is?

The problem is we live too much in our heads, we all *think* too much. *Too busy to live your life?* is about NOT thinking.

It's about escaping the 'stinking thinking', and giving ourselves a break, some space to be and experience *true* meaning in life. It's a big claim, but it is possible, one day at a time.

How? By spending just a few minutes — each day in Nature, *looking* in a new way. All new things need practice and that is why the book is set out as a 28-day journey, following the well-researched theory that it takes 28 days to establish a habit. But, we need to do it every day; it is routine that establishes a habit. That means a few minutes every day, not half an hour once a week.

As children, we learn to name everything we look at, so we can communicate and find our way around this new and exciting world. The trouble is that once we name something, we immediately judge it. We don't let what we are looking at speak for itself. We are no longer 'open' to the truth.

In contrast, when we look without naming, without judging — and simply gaze at something — we start to engage with it. We connect at a deeper level, a heart level. We experience what we are looking at, and that is the key to opening a door on a whole new world of seeing and being.

This is contemplation, or looking with the eyes of the *heart.* In focusing intently on something, we still the mind and enter a different space, a higher level of consciousness, as in meditation. This is where we find solutions to problems that our busy mind finds insurmountable. This is where we get in touch with our inner knowing. We find contentment, fulfilment, purpose and meaning; we discover the treasure within.

This is where we find *happiness.*

When we look in a contemplative way, our awareness expands. Our whole attitude to life starts to change. We can move beyond the judgemental ego-driven mind at any time, and find stillness and peace just by connecting with Nature. When we see the beauty in Nature and connect with it, we start to see the beauty in ourselves.

Somebody once said that we don't think ourselves into a new way of living, we live ourselves into a new way of thinking. *Too busy to live your life?* gives you back the freedom to live your life, today.

I believe that 'we are what we eat' and, as a food writer for many years, I have always been interested in how we can improve our health and also change the way we feel by what we eat.

A year's sabbatical in Asia opened my eyes to the esoteric, aesthetic and medicinal qualities of food. After over 20 years in food, I wondered what the perfect diet for a harmonious life would be. I looked to the monastic world, having experienced this in Japan, and I realised that it is not what monks eat that governs their spiritual condition, it is what they do.
I learned about contemplation.

I understood that being in the day, in the moment, is *essential to wellbeing.* Honouring nature — what St Francis of Assisi and the movement he inspired advocates — is a vital way of connecting to the world and the 'Great Chain of Being'. Too many of us feel we don't belong any more. This causes a spiritual dis-ease that ultimately manifests in physical and mental dis-ease. Connecting with Nature on a regular basis is our medicine for helping us establish a harmonious life.

I have always been looking; seeking something in my life... how to do life better... because I always felt there was more to it. The idea of photographing Nature everyday for a year came to mind as a practical way of experiencing today, every day. It was a test, too, of my self-discipline.

I started to see and experience a world that simply wasn't there for me before.

I could see *beauty* in the most unlikely places. I experienced moments of extreme bliss and calm when focusing on the detail in a flower or the shape of clouds.

I became fascinated by puddles, raindrops and spiders' webs, and admiring their detail transported me beyond my problems and worries. I found my ability to cope with the business and 'busyness' of life improved if I followed my daily discipline of connecting with Nature.

People asked me what I was going to do with the pictures. All I knew was that I wanted to share what I had experienced with other people. What I have learned over the years is the best way to keep something is to give it away. First it was how to cook better — food for the body — now it is how to live better — food for the soul.

My daily blog, 'Walk with Joy' was born. And now, *Too busy to live your life?* A 28-day journey to help you practise looking contemplatively with the daily pictures of Nature, so that when you are out and about during the day, or looking through a window, you will see a change in the way you look at the world. In the 28 days that follow, you will experience a new way of being and you will never look back.

How to 'look' at the daily pictures

Avoid naming anything, as that engages the judgemental mind and the ego – the 'small' self. This practice is about connecting with your big 'true' self.

Allow yourself to become part of the image, to rest within it.

Let your eyes wander slowly within the image. See what catches your attention and connect with it. Study the detail, enjoy it, as if you were going to draw what you have seen or describe it to someone else. Engage with your own wonder; imagine looking at the image as if you are a child.

If the business of your day starts to interfere – how much longer is this going to take, why am I wasting my time doing this or what I am going to cook tonight? – just acknowledge the thoughts and let them float on by.

As in all such disciplines, it is essential to control your breathing. To prepare yourself for gazing at the daily picture, opposite is a short centering and breathing exercise.

Breathing exercise

First, sit down, preferably in a chair that supports your back upright.

Put your feet flat on the floor directly below your knees.
Rock from side to side, to locate your 'sitting bones' beneath each buttock.

Close your eyes. Imagine a thread coming from the top of your head gently lifting up your spine.

Drop your shoulders and allow your head to fall forward slightly.

Breathe out, completely emptying your lungs.

Breathe in from your abdomen, counting slowly until your lungs are filled (3 or 4 should do it), hold it for a couple of seconds.

Exhale slowly, counting out to the same number.

Breathe in and out in this way twice more.

If you want to continue the breathing exercise for longer, you could set a timer for 1-2 minutes; otherwise open your eyes and gaze at the picture.

Allow yourself 2 minutes to start with, and progress to 5 over the next few days.

When our minds are crowded with thoughts, plans, regrets,
projections, ifs and buts and maybes, recognise what's happening.
Nothing.
Why?
Because fear blocks our creativity, our connection to the natural
order, our knowing which way to turn.

That's when we need to stop, walk away and do something entirely
different in order to break that endless churning. That's when we
need to focus on Nature to escape the critical, negative, entirely
egocentric mind, that loves to tell us it's all fantastic or it's all a
disaster. Whichever way, it's not how things truly are.

The non-judgmental, contemplative mind is open, expansive,
compassionate and positive. It's the mind of the child, the mind
of wonder, the mind that takes us deeper into the heart and the
solution.

Nature leads you out of the jungle. Every time. Trust in her.

Gaze and *reflect* today, and allow the solution to present itself

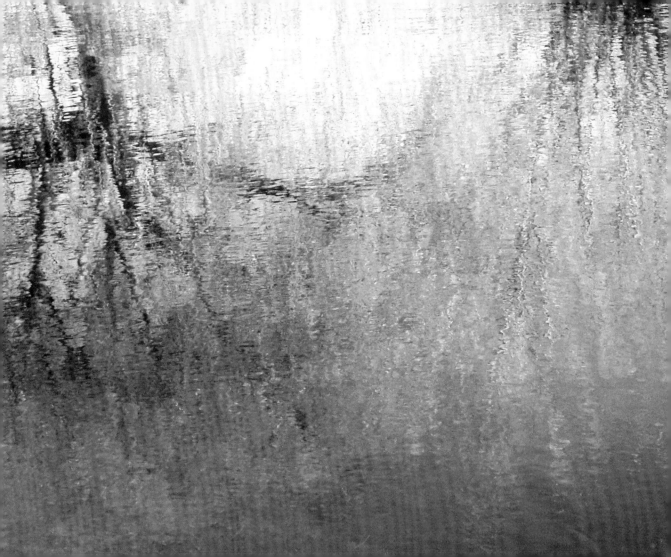

When we get up close to Nature, what we find is beyond amazing. The most delicate, exquisite shapes, forms and colours, finished with the finest brushwork. Detail that would challenge any master-craftsman.

A long single stem of grass supports a head of seeds so intricately balanced they dance in the breeze like a Calder mobile. Abstracted winged seeds connected by threads so fine as to be invisible to all but the silent.

Whatever we spend time with, whenever we focus, this intimate world of Nature is there, revealed, right before our eyes.

We have never seen until we have looked with the eyes of the heart. Experience a world beyond your wildest dreams.

Experience the most beautiful designs in the world, today

The water is so still, the moment is so precious, even breathing might disturb it sleeping beneath the protective film seemingly stretched across its surface. We can't tell where the background of trees finishes and their reflection begins. Reality and illusion blurred by our perception.

A pair of ducks land as if from space with a rude splash. The water responds, sending energetic ripples and scribbles across the whole pond. A dynamic rhythm is established and every tree is drawn in the water.

Slowly the energy fades and the stillness is restored. How quickly do we return to stillness when something out of the blue ruffles our feathers? The more we enter into the stillness, the more we know it is there to call on.

Enter the stillness within *you*, today

All too often our lives are so full that there's no space to move
or breathe. We feel trapped with nowhere to go.

Time to escape and expand into the vast playground that is the sky.
We often forget to look up because we are so preoccupied with the
deeply serious business of our lives. Remember the deep blue of
nothingness, patterned amusingly or exquisitely with all manner
of clouds, is always there, waiting.

As we look more closely, the joy of seeing the moon at play during
the day reminds us life is about living, experiencing, and being in
the moment.

Experience the sky, today

A narrow track leads through the long grass, inviting, beckoning.
We are drawn towards the mystery, the substance, the meaning of life.

At a certain time for all of us the shiny things start to lose their lustre.
There is something missing.
Happiness, stillness, fulfilment, understanding?
Why save Heaven until this journey is over when Nature shows us
that it's here, right now.

All we need to do is take the path towards the light.
Acknowledge that we are willing to grow, and to experience life in all
its fullness. Here's to taking that path now.

Let Nature beckon you, today

The bulrushes gather around, bending in unison in the breeze,
as if protecting something precious.

It brings back childhood memories of the harrowing bible story of
Moses and his mother, willing to entrust her baby to God and the
bulrushes, rather than risk certain death at the hands of the Pharaoh.

We often face difficult decisions that test our faith and require us to
trust in the unknown. When we are willing to trust the Universe to
support us, and learn to accept the outcome, we can step aside from
any fear that holds us back.

Nature helps us connect with our core faith and to experience being
supported by something bigger than ourselves.

When we know that we are loved and supported no matter what,
we are free to walk without fear, to walk with joy.

Trust that you are supported, *no matter what*, today

Stop for a moment and imagine the leaves falling singly and gracefully from the trees. With no wind they take their time, returning to the earth to provide soil for future generations. It's all so poetically complete.

Several leaves collect in the big bough of the tree, vast and womb-like, comprising nine large trunks. The sun is now high enough to announce itself, bringing to life anything in its path. It's like looking into a crucible, as if the alchemist himself is going to transform these copper and gold leaves into the real thing.

Awesome and other worldly, there's a feeling that anything could happen, anything is possible and, indeed, when we connect with the power of Nature and the power of the Universe, it is.

Allow the power of Nature to awaken your inner power, today

When we allow ourselves to be drawn and not driven, we allow our inner selves to open up and experience the mystery, the unexpected and the enchanted.

And so taking an unknown path under a heavy grey sky, the park becomes a jungle of giant undiscovered trees snaking sideways overhead. Curtains of leaves suspended above us diffuse the light and cast a magical green haze in the damp air. Only the creaking of the trees can be heard until a pair of screeching parakeets completes the tropical illusion.

Lost in wonder. Lost in praise. Lost all worries.
Another world within this world, another way to experience,
another way to be.

Be drawn into the unexpected, today

The sea is so still it's as if a pastel-coloured chiffon scarf holds the water in place. Only a thin white line marks the horizon, otherwise there is nothing.

It is hypnotic and mesmerisingly beautiful.
There is no sense of space or time, past or future.
But there is a sense that the water could draw you into the sea mist forever.

Giant white boulders as smooth as waves emerge from the sand.
A single pure white stone separates land from sky and invites total focus.

Rejuvenating, transforming, unforgettable.

Find stillness in *purity*, today

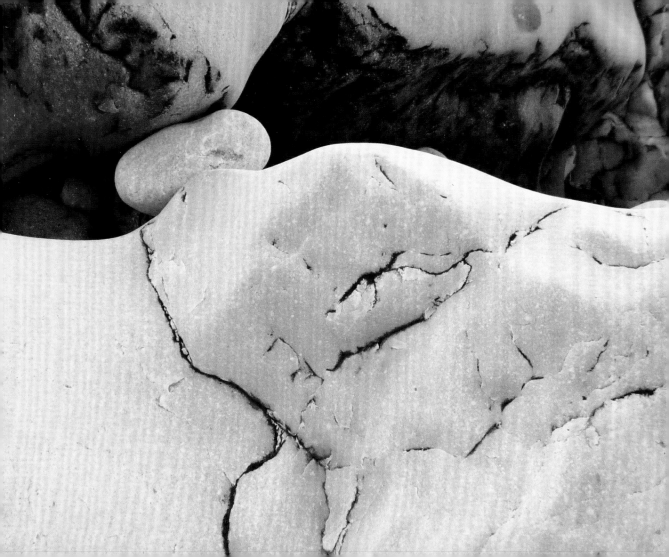

The morning arrives.
Deep shafts of light dance through the trees.
Try and catch them and they are gone, like finding the end of
a rainbow.

Four snowy white-breasted gulls walk the muddy bank, then launch
themselves silently into the grey of the water. A low haze makes
everything seem very ethereal. The gulls preen, paddle, stand
motionless, making perfect reflections in the water and interlocking
web prints in the mud.

All worldly concerns have drifted away as the delightful dance of the
gulls plays on below. Nothing matters, apart from it would be good to
catch a worm, and even that will happen when it's time.

And then, like the dancing rays of light, they are gone.

Be part of *the dance*, today

Water collected on the path has frozen overnight, preserving everything for us to admire. A pair of plane tree leaves, touchingly close, are held top to tail. The ice is as clear as glass, apart from the tiniest of bubbles. Each leaf echoes the movement of the other, in harmony.

When we step aside from our individual egos and desires and work together, life is harmonious.

Many have famously said, 'Man is not an island'; time to remember there are others who inhabit our world.

Nature reminds us we are not the *only one*, today

When we stop and admire, Nature always invites us in.
Another veil is dropped, another layer revealed.
Something we have never seen before.

It's like being in love; everything is wonderful, precious and special.
The world is a delight and we delight in it all.

When we admire Nature, the love affair lasts forever.

Fall in love with Nature, today

The way to finding our centre is challenging.
We have to negotiate obstacles, deal with disappointment, trauma
and crises. Often the light is obscured, we can't see where we are
going and we lose our way in the cloud.

As free spirits, we have choices.
To trust and keep on walking into obscurity or to lose faith,
turn back and never arrive.

When we take the leap of faith and trust, we let go of old behaviour
and baggage and allow the power of the Universe to work within us.

Then we see a way through and we start to know who guides us and
who we truly are.

Trust, follow your heart and you will *find the way*, today

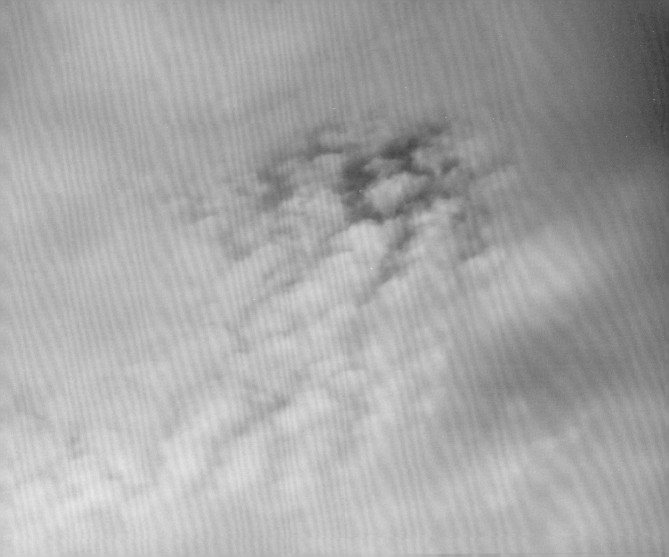

The most important thing we can do today is celebrate life.
It's too easy to take it all for granted and miss out because we are
preoccupied, worrying about yesterday and what we didn't do,
and fretting about tomorrow and how we can fit it all in.
All what?

We are too busy being busy, being driven by 'got to', 'should' and 'must'.
Whatever happened to 'I am here, as I am'?

Nature is celebrating right now. We can't miss the riot of colour and
ripening fruits, or can we? One thing is true – when we stop and admire
Nature, we feel alive, connected to an energy that is infinitely more
exciting and lasting.

Tap into the power of Nature and find the hope, strength and courage
to carry on, whatever is happening in our lives.

Celebrate Nature, *celebrate* life, today

When we have our eyes fully open we see so much more, we stop to admire and find beauty in the simplest, most ordinary things.

Two stones on the path, lumps of flint, shaped like dinosaur vertebrae, perhaps created at the same time. Deep long shadows make them more important, as if in the spotlight, demanding attention.

Circular swirls in the concrete become apparent as we focus, patterns left by a human hand.
A study in stillness... unexpected and delightful.
A moment in time, lasting in its simplicity.

Gone tomorrow, but forever remembered.

Honour simplicity, today

How often does something so utterly beautiful render you
speechless?

Allowing ourselves to gaze at some twigs in a pond transports us
to a world beyond words — layers of beauty appear gradually as
we are drawn deeper and deeper.

Tiny bubbles form around the bark, last autumn's leaves rest beneath
the surface, reflections zigzag across the water — Nature's calligraphy
changing with the wind.

Time stops for us.
Suddenly we are nowhere, not feeling anything, in nothingness, and
we only realise this when our awareness returns.

This ineffable, inexplicable, indescribable state is contemplation.
The world beyond words, where we can centre ourselves in the
stillness and experience the wisdom within.
All without knowing.

Beauty often defies description and it is the door through which
we enter the mystery.

Stop and experience the silence of beauty, today

Slender, bare beech trees, some so close together
they are almost touching, as if in tender conversation.

The atmosphere certainly feels intimate, awakened,
expressive and alive.
There is no defence, no barrier to communication.
Everything feels real, safe and true.
In truth it is.

The trees in the light, glowing, breathing.
Simply expressing and radiating their energy.
Being themselves, being beautiful.

Reminding us we are too.

Be *still* and see what you hear, today

When we engage with Nature, we move out of our 'small', isolated self and become part of the Universal energy. It's like coming home. We feel safe, light and free to be who we are meant to be.

It is a moment for all our senses to connect, kick off our shoes, feel the sand between our toes, lie down in the grass, gaze up into the branches of a magnificent oak or follow a bee as it explores deep into the bell of a flower.

As Man becomes more and more detached from Nature he becomes more and more detached from his 'big', real self. We run around in circles trying to find the secret of life only to find the more we run, the more lost and disenchanted we become.

When we stop, breathe and be quiet for just a moment, the world comes to us.
It's then we realise we have arrived, we were there all the time.
We don't need to run any more because the secret lies within.
Nature shows us how to get there.

Let Nature guide you inside, today

Long grass sways in more directions than there seem directions, iridescent, diaphanous, so filled with light it becomes invisible. Suddenly it is back again, stems as green as a child's paint box, feathery tops scattered with seeds – sewn in by fairies, no doubt.

Filled with gratitude at experiencing such beauty, the grass seemingly hears, and in an instant reveals another, richer layer of magic.

Express your gratitude, today

After the rain, the light is crystal.
Everything is sharply defined.
It's as if layers have been washed away, revealing how life truly is.

The seed heads of dandelions filter the sun's rays,
splitting the spectrum and scattering colour like rainbow dust.

Only whole for a moment, they invite us to blow their seeds and
wonder about time in a moment that is endlessly precious.

Let Nature invite you to spend *time* with her, today

The London plane tree grows by shedding its bark like the skin of a snake, exposing the tender yellow ochre skin below.

The trunk becomes a canvas of subtle natural pigments, from silver grey through to sage green and pale tan, in random swirls and circles like a topographic map in camouflage.

When we practise seeing with the eyes of the heart, we see beauty without even trying. It becomes our normal way of viewing the world.

The more delights we find, the more delightful we become; the more beauty we see, the more beauty we reflect.

See the beauty in the *detail*, today

In sharp contrast to the riot of colour all around it,
the monochromatic pond talks softly.
Something about the gentle curve of the ripples
— understated, evenly spaced, there and not there — draws us in.

Thoughts tumbling round and round untangle themselves and float
away. All the time the ripples soften, the breath stills and deepens.

There is no separation, there is no observer and observed anymore,
only the sensation of being lulled into a timeless space of stillness.

Of wholeness. Of calm. Of being.

Become the stillness, today

Where do we escape from the heat of the day, under a tree, from
a shower of rain, under a tree, from being caught in hide and seek,
behind a tree, the madness in your head?
You guessed it.
We can change what we feel by changing what we focus on.

Choose a tree, for example, watch it move in the wind, follow the
shadow it casts. Identify with its movement — effortless, willing and
joyful. Imagine going about the day with the same energy.

Whilst we are enjoying the tree, all thoughts of self disappear.
The mind becomes quiet and gives us space to be.
Not surprisingly, our energy is mirrored by what we are focusing on.

We become willing and joyful, effortlessly.

Escape to the world of Nature, today.

Man, with no natural predators apart from man, places himself near the top of the Great Chain of Being, the classical categorisation of Universal life from algae to the Divine.

Our dominance turned superiority has separated us from the rest, from Nature, from the Universal energy. Many spiritual leaders believe this has created a malaise in many people, an indefinable yet deep sense of dis-ease.

When we actively connect with Nature, we belong, we are part, and we share in that Universal energy.
We start to care and protect.
We have purpose.
We are supported by the Great Chain of Being and we understand that whatever is at the bottom of the chain is as important as that at the top.

Everything matters, all we have to do is remember that.

Be part of the *Great Chain of Being*, today

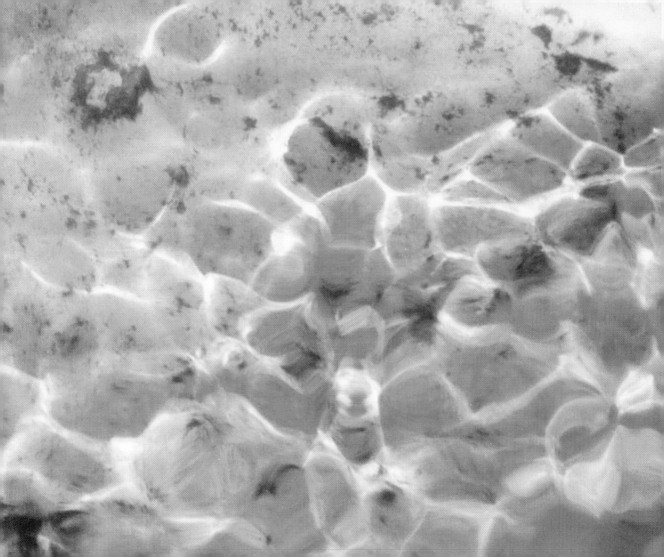

What looked like a dusting of white blossom at the edge of a shady
lawn turned out to be something more magical, a carpet of daisies.
Kneeling down amongst them immediately transports us to the land of
daisy chains and 'he loves me, he loves me not'.
Absolute honesty to the last petal.

Their cartoon-like snowy-white heads stretch towards the light,
showing off their shocking pink petticoat petals.
Sheer childhood delight.

A forgotten world revisited.
Lost in a world of innocence, simplicity and wonder.

Remember life can be simple; *keep it simple*, today

When our world is turned upside down, we are forced to look at
things differently. We might feel uncomfortable, even in pain or lost.
Certainly the more fixed we are, the more challenging we find change.
Yet it is only through change that we grow.
We have to open our eyes.

The same thing happens when we look into a puddle.
How a couple of centimetres of water can change everything.
What we see is often unexpected.

Our awareness is awakened and the water becomes a door into
another world, where colours fuse, edges blur and lamp posts distort
as the wind stirs the surface.

We are reminded to look up at the clouds racing past and the crow
which has just swooped by.

We appreciate what is under our noses so much more because a
shower of rain has created a mirror at our feet

Be **prepared** to *enter another world*, today

Deep, deep blueness that stretches to infinity.
A feeling of total freedom.
Abandonment.
Stillness.
Falling into the emptiness of a blank canvas with two playful
wisps of Cirrus.

It feels as if we could pull the blue cloak of sky around us and
be transported. All thoughts of smallness disappear in the sheer
vastness of the scene.

Admire the majestic Scots pine, bold and shapely; follow its slender
trunk up to the sky.
Feel exhilarated, as if you're a bird about to spread its wings and fly.

Let the vastness of the sky take your *spirit* for a *ride*, today

A short distance from the razzmatazz of an overcrowded seaside town on a sunny Saturday, with its chaotic mix of roaring motorbikes, funfair-ride tunes and overheated voices, there is another world.

Away from the crowds, the sound of the wind and the waves expands the space rather than diminishes it. Trillions of the tiniest mussels are edged into the rocks at every angle. The water carves feather patterns in the sand. Giant lumps of seawall concrete focus the eye to a small pool and the smooth, rippled pattern etched into the sandstone since time began.

So elemental. So other planet. So other time, in an instant. All it takes is one glance towards the light.

When we remove ourselves from the noise, we give ourselves a chance to see the beauty amidst the chaos. The everlasting behind the temporal. We can take time to rebalance and realise what matters most.

Let Nature remind you what *matters*, today

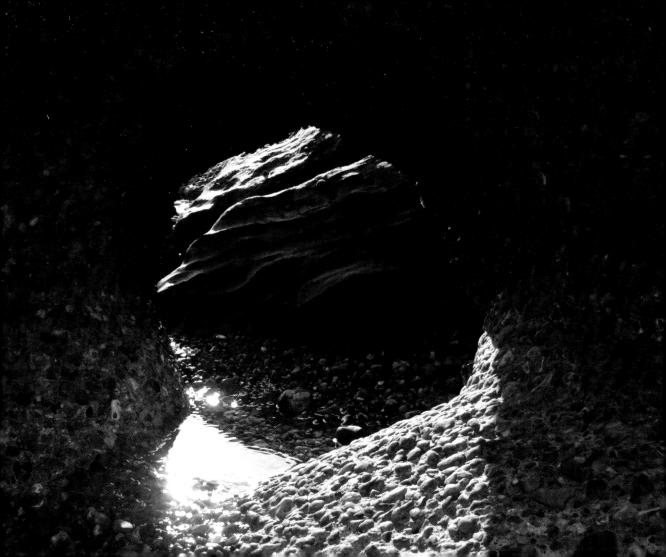

I dedicate this book to all those who are seeking to create a more harmonious world

Contemplation is an experience that I encourage you to explore from now on, by spending time with Nature, daily. Allow the eyes of the heart to be your guide and walkwithjoy.com your companion.

ACKNOWLEDGEMENTS

I would like to thank designer Lawrence Morton for believing in my idea and bringing it to life so beautifully. Lewis Esson too, my editor, who made sure the words were in the right order and we didn't break too many grammatical rules. Lynda Graham, business whiz kid and lifelong friend who reminded me that 28 days can change your life. Most of all, my partner, Gareth Jones, who continues to encourage and support in more ways than I can mention.

Thanks to both, Huw and Tom, our sons, for saying, 'it's all good.'

Many have supported my daily blog walkwithjoy.com, from which this 28-day journey was compiled, offering advice and encouragement, notably (in alphabetical order) Sharon Aldersley, Tracey Bradley, Alice Cacouris, Peter Crosskey, Ruth Dent, Sarah Forss, Janie Joel, Gerald 'Gez' Lamb, Sharron Lister and Joe O'Toole. Thank you all.

First published in 2012 by Walk with Joy
enquiries@walkwithjoy.com

Text and photography © 2012 Joy Davies

Design and layout © 2012 Lawrence Morton

Edited by Lewis Esson

The rights of the author have been asserted.

Cataloguing in Publication Data: a catalogue record for this book is available from the British Library.

ISBN 978-0-9571177-0-9

Printed in United Kingdom by Aldgate Press Ltd London